The worlball humor, star of humorists:

BO McMILh's doghouse anant McMillin!' "

JIM TATUM—"in his first game as a Tarheel, winding up with a funny-bone bruise."

KNUTE ROCKNE—"how the funniest coach of them all handled sullen alumni, wise-cracking reporters, and hard-bitten linemen."

JOHNNY LUJACK—"telling his coach why so many of his passes were intercepted by the Army safety man."

JIM THORPE—"it seems that an opposing lineman was giving Jim the 'business' until Jim tapped the fellow on his helmet and . . ."

STEVE OWEN—"the time the Bears started ripping the jerseys off the Giants' backs."

EDDIE LeBARON—"chopping the big fellows down to his size at the training table."

HERMAN HICKMAN—"making piles as a sophomore."

JIMMY CONZELMAN—"all about Biter Jones, who bit eleven guards, two centers, and snapped at a house mother."

★   ★   ★

Cover by Willard Mullin

SPORTS STORY COLLECTOR

Herman L. Masin, author, has a million of 'em—side-splitting sports stories, that is. Well, maybe not a million, but plenty! At any rate, he's been collecting these gems for years and years—ever since he became editor of *Scholastic Coach*.

This technical sports publication is one of the *Scholastic* family of magazines for students and educators, and is read regularly by practically all the coaches and athletic directors in the colleges and high schools of the United States. The most popular department in it is "Coaches' Corner," where many of these stories first appeared.

Mr. Masin also writes the popular sports section in *Scholastic* magazines—*Senior Scholastic, World Week, Practical English,* and *Junior Scholastic*—and is author of three treasures of sports humor. He has also written articles for many outstanding publications and has authored at least fifty instructional sports booklets for young players and coaches.

If you like this book, you'll be interested in several other SBS books on sports written by the same author. These are *How to Star in Basketball, How to Star in Football, How to Star in Baseball,* and *Baseball Laughs.*

for LAUGHING out LOUD

by HERMAN L. MASIN

Editor, *Scholastic Coach*

Cover by Willard Mullin

Cartoons by Doug Anderson

CHOLASTIC BOOK SERVICES

Published by Scholastic Book Services, a division
of Scholastic Magazines, Inc., New York, N. Y.

Copyright 1954 by Scholastic Corporation. This edition is published by Scholastic Book Services, a division of Scholastic Magazines, Inc.

9th printing......................September 1968

Printed in the U.S.A.

Forward Pass

PEOPLE LOOKING FOR LAUGHS turn on the TV, take in a movie, or pick up a comic book. They *don't* go to football games. No, sir! The pigskin pastime isn't built for chuckles. It's a deadly serious business where irresistible forces are always running into immovable objects. And anytime you have 11 fellows weighing about a ton apiece striking 11 other fellows weighing ditto, you can hardly expect any humor sparks to fly.

Yet funny things DO happen on the prison-striped field of battle. Bring any 22 healthy young beasts together for two hours and we don't care what they do—play checkers, clobber each other, or sing Christmas carols—they'll find something to laugh about. This quality—or ability to see the humorous side of things—is as American as yo-yos and Boston beans, and we're a richer nation because of it.

The chief historian of these comic turns is the coach. On the field, in the locker room, at assemblies and banquets, the coach is always telling about the funny things his players said or did. Some coaches are four-alarm riots as storytellers. They can take a funny incident, give it a little twist, and roll you in the aisles with it.

Other coaches aren't so fortunately blessed. But all own a fund of rib-ticklers. Stick any coach in front of an audience and he'll spout gems of the purest (b)ray serene.

The gems, or anecdotes, in this book represent the cream of an 18-year crop. That's how long it took to collect them. They've been culled from books, newspapers, magazines, letters, conversations, speeches, movies, and little birdies.

If you've heard some of them before with different individuals as their heroes, don't blame the writer. Coaches love to pick up a good story and switch it around to suit themselves. All is fair in war and humor, and nobody ever screams foul.

All right then: ready for the kick-off? Toot! Let's go.

HERMAN MASIN

Kickoff

ALBIE BOOTH, Yale's immortal "Little Boy Blue," was a sensation in his senior year —until the Elis ran into a wheed-up Georgia eleven. The great Georgia end, Catfish Smith, stopped little Albie cold. He kept hitting him harder and harder, until Booth blew his top.

"Now listen, Smith," he yelped, "there are a couple of things that don't go around here and roughness is one of them."

"Sure," drawled the Catfish, "and you're the other."

———————

Clemson was playing Mercer back in 1934, and with the game practically over the referee turned to Streak Lawton, Clemson halfback, and said: "Streak, this is the last game of the season and you have just 60 seconds left to make history."

Just then, Mercer punted and Lawton dashed 90 yards to a score. He raced back up the field, tossed the ball to the referee, and gasped: "What are the other 40 seconds for, mister?"

The slippery little halfback tried to find a hole in the strong side of the Oklahoma line. Four monsters hit him at once. The doctor and the trainer rushed out. They discovered a broken leg, a fractured arm, a concussion, and a sprained wrist.

A half-hour later, the boy opened his eyes. "Does it hurt much?" the doctor asked.

The boy shook his head. "Only when I laugh," he said.

When Doc Spears was coaching at Wisconsin, he wasn't particularly noted for coddling his players. One afternoon a member of the athletic board approached him and said, "Coach Spears, why is it the boys don't love you the way they do other coaches?"

The rough and rugged Doc eyed the gent. "Professor," he retorted, "I've been too darn busy coaching to do much courting."

The coach was annoyed at his star full-back. All during the skull session the prima donna sat in the corner of the room engrossed in a comic book. The coach said nothing. But next Saturday, the star fullback found himself on the bench. He sat there for three full periods. In the middle of the fourth quarter, with the game reaching a crucial point, the coach finally called upon him. "Warm up," he ordered.

The fullback began doing push-ups, knee bends, and practice charges. Finally the coach called him over.

"Are you ready?" he asked tensely.

"Yes, sir!" panted the fullback.

"Okay," snapped the coach. "Here's a comic book. Start reading!"

A couple of kids playing football in a vacant lot kicked the pigskin into a nearby chicken yard. The rooster, puzzled, sidled up to it. Firmly convinced of what he saw, he ran over to the hen house and stuck his head in the door.

"Hey, you gals," he cackled, "think you're pretty hot, eh? Well get a load of what they're turning out in the next yard!"

Moon Mullins, the old Notre Damer who turned to coaching, was a disciplinarian in the tradition of Knute Rockne. He was dead set against smoking and told his players so. One day he came around a corner and spied one of his boys frozen against the wall, a lighted cigarette at his feet.

"What about that cigarette?" he demanded.

"You can have it, Coach," the boy said. "You saw it first."

———

The dumb football player kept pleading, "Coach, send me in! Lemme at 'em! Lemme get in there, woncha?" The coach held up a hand, "Aw, stop bothering me. Why don't you go across the field and talk to the coach of your own team?"

———

The iron-ribbed, oak-headed backfield star was taking his first classroom exam. He answered every question—wrong. The professor called him to his office and, pointing to his paper, said: "I don't believe you know anything."

"Sir, I don't even suspect anything," the boy replied.

When Bo McMillin was quarterbacking the famous Praying Colonels of Centre College, he once fell into disfavor with his coach, Charley Moran. Saturday came around, and Bo still lingered in the doghouse. In the third quarter, the fans started yelling, "We want McMillin!"

This went on for some time until Moran finally beckoned to Bo. McMillin ripped off his hood and began limbering up on the sideline. "Who do I go in for, Coach?" he asked.

"You're not going *in*," snapped Charley. "You're going *up*—in the stands with your friends. They want you more than I do."

Eddie Dooley, the old Dartmouth All-American, likes to tell about the trick play he rigged up against Harvard. The idea was to fake a couple of times, then fade back and throw a 50-yard pass to a man free in the end zone.

The day of the game came and Harvard forged ahead by six points. Try as it might, Dartmouth couldn't push the ball over. With three minutes to play, Dartmouth recovered a fumble on the 50-yard line. "Here," thought Eddie, "is the time for my play."

He called the signal—the fakes went off

faultlessly—Eddie faded back—lifted his arm to pass—and was smothered for a 25-yard loss. Undaunted, he called his signal again. Again everything went off smoothly—until Eddie lifted his arm. This time he was pulled down on his three-yard line.

As Eddie lined up for the next play, a raucous voice floated out of the bleachers. "Will somebody give that moron a ticket— he may want to get back in the stadium after the next play."

Several years ago Yale had a fine guard by the name of Jablonski, who played both ways with nary a rest. One afternoon a powerful Cornell team started running wild over the Elis. The Cornell coach began pouring in second- and third-stringers to keep the score down, but to no avail.

Jablonski stayed in there all the time, battling three fresh guards. Finally the fourth-stringer came in. All fired up, he started chanting, "Come on, come on, let's kill this guy!"—meaning Jablonski.

Jablonski looked up wearily and sighed, "Aw, shut up. If you're so good, you'd have been in here a long time ago."

"What's the new halfback's name?" asked the coach.

"Osscowinsinsiski," replied his assistant.

"Good," exclaimed the coach with satisfaction. "Put him on the first team. Boy, will I get even with those newspaper reporters!"

———

Statue of Liberty Play

Georgia Tech was playing a tough opponent one afternoon, and the only desire the Engineers had was to escape with life and limb. They went into a huddle and the quarterback called a fullback smash over center.

"Don't run that one," mumbled the fullback. "Last time we tried it that backer-up almost twisted my neck off."

"Well, all right," said the quarterback. "We'll send the left half around end."

"Don't do that," said the left half. "Last time that end nearly broke my leg."

"Okay," said the quarterback, "the right half around left end."

"Oh, no," cracked the right half. "Last time that guy broke a couple of my ribs."

"Well," asked the quarterback, completely stumped, "what shall we do?"

"I know," replied a guard, "let's throw a nice, long, incomplete pass."

———————

A sportswriter asked Ray Eliot why he changed his name from Nusspickel to Eliot. He got an instant answer. "Wouldn't it sound terrible," the former Illinois coach said, "to hear the stands give three cheers and a locomotive for Nusspickel!"

Coach Forest Evashevski was asked what type of offense Michigan State would use against his Iowa team. "It'll be 70% Michigan single wing, 15% split T, and 13% straight T," Evashevski answered.

"That's only 98%," it was pointed out to him. "What about the other 2%?"

"Sales tax," explained the Hawkeye coach.

———

Ron Drzewiecki, Marquette halfback, strutted back into the huddle after making a perfect block in the Cincinnati game. He turned to quarterback Dick Shockey and asked how he liked it. "It was great," the signal caller said, "but you were supposed to carry the ball on that play!"

———

Al Davis, the head coach of the Oakland Raiders, was guest speaker at a football dinner. As he rose to his feet, a news photographer started jockeying for a good angle. The toastmaster, fearing that Al would be annoyed, snapped at the photographer: "Don't take his picture while he's speaking. Shoot him before he starts."

The visiting team was having a bad afternoon. Everything they tried went wrong. Their passes were intercepted, their line bucks were smeared, and their reverses were smothered. The captain signalled desperately to the coach, "What should we do now?"

The coach immediately signalled back, "Try fumbling."

———

Bill Fay, a magazine writer, polled 1,247 college football players for their opinion of the one-platoon system. One of the men answered the seven questions, signed his name, then scribbled: "I have neither given nor received aid in taking this examination."

———

Subway alumni—they're wonderful! Our favorite specimen is the fellow who attended a Colgate-Syracuse game some years ago. Though he had never been within 1,000 miles of Colgate, he stood up when the alma mater was played.

When asked why he rose, he explained: "Maybe I never went to Colgate, but I've always used their toothpaste."

One of those old-time coaches now teaching Sunday school never muffed a chance to ring in some resounding grid terms, leading some members of the congregation to feel that he was dispensing football lore at the cost of religion.

One day two parishioners were listening to him hold forth. "Where is he?" asked one, consulting the text for the day.

"I think," observed the other, "he's got the Devil on the 20-yard line."

———————

It's been Coach Fritz Brennecke's custom at the Colorado School of Mines to call the roll the first few days in order to familiarize himself with the names of the boys. The weather around Golden, Colorado, is pretty hot in early September; but like most coaches, Brennecke drives his lads pretty hard.

One afternoon he called the name of Lee, but nobody answered. "Lee?" he repeated. Again no answer. "Anybody know where Lee is?" the coach asked. There was a moment of silence before someone spoke up, "Coach, I think he's getting married this afternoon."

From the outer fringes of the group came a tired drawl, "Some guys will go to any lengths to get out of practice around here."

During a Harvard game several seasons ago, the badly beaten Crimson called one of its numerous times out. The student manager grabbed his water bucket, rushed on the field, and politely asked the nearest official, "May I go in now, sir?"

"Yeah," the whistle-tooter replied, "I thought the coach was about ready to send you in."

———

Jim Tatum, the late Maryland coach, was a big country boy when he arrived at the University of North Carolina to play football. In his first game as a Tarheel, he was getting a fierce going-over in the line. Hurt and bewildered, he turned to the veteran end, Erwin Walker, and asked, "What should I do?"

"Well," Walker told him, "I'll tip off the official to watch what's happening to you. Then you call this guy across from you a name. He's sure to slug you, and they'll be penalized 15 yards. You're willing to take just one sock on the nose for the old alma mater, aren't you, Jim?"

So Tatum got down in the line and glared at the guy across from him. "You big lug," he snarled. Bang! The guy let him have it.

Poor Tatum fell down, rolled around on the ground, then slowly rose. He looked at Walker. "Well, what happened?" he mumbled.

"We scored on the play," his pal told him, "and had to decline the penalty."

During the 1951 Mississippi-Tulane game, Buck Buchanan of Ole Miss snatched a Tulane fumble in mid-air and took off for the promised land. Upon reaching the Mississippi bench, he swerved toward the sidelines and yelled:

"Hey, Coach, send Buddy Bowen in, quick. I'm only the defensive quarterback."

Football coaches on the west coast were discussing the feasibility of adding a fifth official for all games. Moving to a blackboard, Coach Kip Taylor of Oregon State outlined the territory which the extra official would cover. Then a thought occurred to him. "What'll we call him?" he wondered.

"Hmmm," rasped Jim Aiken, then coach of Oregon. "You'll probably call him a blankety-blank just like you do the other four."

Something Old,
Something Knute

COACHES UNANIMOUSLY AGREE that the greatest yarn spinner of them all was Knute Rockne. The old master of blocks and tackles had a repertoire longer than Sammy Baugh's passing record.

Our pet Rockne yarn is the one about his experience with soccer. Sold on the possibilities of the game as a conditioner, he tried introducing it in preseason training. He described the game as best he could, winding up with, "The main idea of soccer is to kick the ball or kick the other fellow's shins."

So the boys chose up sides and lined up for the kick-off. Whereupon they discovered they had no ball. The boys mulled this over for a moment, then a big lineman drawled, "Heck with the ball, Rock! Let's start the game!"

In his earlier years at Notre Dame, Rockne used to swear like a trooper. One of the regular visitors at practice was Father Hennessy. But Rock's language never bothered him. One afternoon Rockne let fly with a particularly loud and salty oath. Everybody immediately turned to Father Hennessy.

"Oh, glory be to God," he intoned, clearly enough for Rockne to hear. "There goes Rockne saying his prayers again!"

———————

Hunk Anderson and Knute Rockne made a delightful combination at Notre Dame. While Hunk would be driving the guards and tackles, Rock would be coddling the ends and backs.

When Rock was ready for some scrimmage, he would call: "Heartley, old fellow, would you mind bringing the behemoths over?" Anderson would go right on hounding and sweating the linemen.

"Heartley," Rock would call again, "could we trouble you for the use of your monsters?" Still no answer, and Rock would call again.

Finally Hunk would holler, "Aw, wait a while, Rock. These guys ain't even bleedin' yet."

In addition to all his other talents, Rockne
was a master diplomat. Once a weak Minnesota team unexpectedly held the Irish to a
tie. Stomping out of the stadium in a rage,
Rock was intercepted by a stranger, who demanded: "What's the matter with your
team? It stinks."

Rock whirled on him. "Did you pay to get
in?"

"Did I pay to get in!" The man fished into
a pocket and brought out a fistful of ticket
stubs.

Rock looked at the stubs glumly. "You're
right," he said. "We stink."

———

When Rockne was coaching the Four
Horsemen, he devised a beauty of a play
which pulled both guards as well as the center to run interference for the ball-carrier.
The chap who was supposed to protect the
huge gap in the middle was the quarterback,
Harry Stuhldreher.

"How did it work, Rock?" asked an interested fellow coach to whom the Notre Dame
mastermind was explaining the play.

"I dunno," confessed Rockne sadly. "You
don't think Stuhldreher was ever silly enough
to call the play, do you?"

When Rockne was building Notre Dame football, his main concern was a representative schedule. He appealed to Bob Zuppke for a game with Illinois. But Zup found little enchantment in the idea. He pointed out that the Irish were unbeaten, that they were a dangerous team without a national reputation.

Whereupon Rockne replied, "But I'm losing my first team through graduation." Zuppke remained unmoved. Rockne continued, "I'm also losing my second team through graduation."

"Sorry, Rock," retorted Zup, ending the conversation, "but I don't think your third team would draw in Champaign!"

Although Rockne was of Norwegian ancestry, he was known as "The Swede" at Notre Dame. Only once was he bettered in a word duel, and that by Sleepy Jim Crowley.

Crowley was having trouble learning an assignment and Rockne, growing impatient, lashed out at him. "Can you name anyone," he growled, "dumber than a dumb Irishman?"

"Yes," retorted Crowley, sweetly, "a smart Swede."

The Swede got the worst of it on another occasion, but since it was through an honest error it never counted against his record. That was when he was introduced to the late Heywood Broun. Rockne had just turned out an undefeated football team at Notre Dame and Broun was at the height of his brilliant newspaper career on the *New York World*.

"Glad to meet you," exclaimed the dynamic Rock. "I never miss a line of your stuff in the *Journal*."

"Thank you, Mr. Rockne," retorted Broun gravely. "And let me tell you that I always enjoy seeing your Yale basketball teams."

Delayed Buck

During the 1939 Rice-LSU game, the ball flew back and forth in crazy fashion, with interceptions and completed passes galore. Sitting in the stands was Jim Crowley, a solid believer in fundamental football—hard blocking, savage tackling, strict attention to the ground game.

A reporter nearby asked him, "What do you think of the game, Jim?"

Crowley thought for a moment. "Well," he said, "the game sure has speeded up a lot since they eliminated the center jump."

———

Knute was once asked to give the main requisite of a perfect football player. Rockne pondered a few minutes, then solemnly declared:

"I'd say the perfect football player would be a left halfback who was cross-eyed and could pass with either hand!"

———

Girls who go to games to eat
   And moan of chilly hands and feet
And never stop that moving jaw,
   Will be asked to games no more.
   —Unless they're beautiful!

Of all the Rockne-ophytes who went on to become famous coaches and storytellers in their own right, Crowley came closest to the old master in delivery and humor. The ex-Fordham coach was one of the Four Horsemen at Notre Dame and something of a good-time charley. At least, that's what his pet yarn would have you believe.

Notre Dame has always enforced a strict midnight curfew. One night in Jim's sophomore year, he happened to be roaming around in downtown South Bend. Although it was almost midnight, he was going anywhere but back to school, which was two and a half miles from town.

Turning a corner, he walked right into the arms of the dean in charge of discipline. The dean glanced at his watch and then looked at Crowley coldly. It was two minutes to midnight.

"James, you know you're due back at school," he said.

"Not until 12 o'clock, Father," retorted Crowley.

"Well," said the dean, "do you think you can make it?"

Crowley pondered a moment, then without flickering an eyelash, he murmured. "Not against this wind, Father."

Crowley's answer to Pearl Harbor was to quit his post at Fordham and enlist in the Navy. While attending the V-5 Instructor's School at the Naval Academy, he was called upon to maneuver his section out of the gym. The section was headed straight for the bleachers, and Crowley couldn't remember the command that would straighten them out.

In desperation, he roared orders never heard on a parade ground. He finally stopped the section by exclaiming, "Left, right, or something. But for heaven's sake fellers, don't go up the bleachers!"

———

A situation always loaded with humorous possibilities is that following a knockout block or tackle. Before permitting a flattened player to continue, most coaches make certain he's in full command of his senses. A few simple questions determine this.

Perhaps the classic quiz story concerns the coach who has just seen the breath knocked out of his star quarterback. Smelling salts revive the player; then, to play safe, the coach asks him if he knows his plays. The boy rattles off his assignments perfectly. Satisfied, the coach tells him to go ahead and call the plays.

"Coach, I can't," the boy announces.

The coach looks at him with surprise, "Why not? Are you hurt?"

"No, Coach, I'm ineligible."

Epitaph

Here lies the body of Fullback Bill,
For him life held no terror,
Tried to climb the Army line—
No hits, no runs, one error.

I shot a pass into the air,
It fell to earth I know not where;
And that is why I sit and dream
On the bench with the second team.

Sleepy Jim and an Iowa tackle named Jones could well have been brothers under the pigskin. Jones is the hero of Forest Evashevski's favorite story.

When Evashevski arrived at Iowa as head coach, he inherited a team with a losing complex. A keen student of human nature, Evashevski worked hard to cure his players' defeatist attitude. He drove them from early noon to twilight, then lectured them in the squad room.

During one of his lectures on line play, he kept harping on the importance of the tackles. "Most football games," he declared, "are lost at the tackles, either just inside or just outside the tackles."

Looking up, he noticed one of his tackles snoozing in the back row. "Jones!" he roared, "Where are most football games lost?"

Quick as a flash Jones retorted, "Right here at Iowa, Coach!"

———

Halfbacks who run like pelicans
Never wind up All-Americans.

Umbrella Defense

Steaming 'Em Up

PEP TALKS CONSTITUTE another lush source of coaching humor. Very close to the top on every pep parade is the one credited to Mal Stevens when the suave, witty doctor was coaching at Yale.

It seemed that his puny Eli team was taking a pasting from Harvard and some half-time inspiration was obviously in order.

"Gentlemen," Mal intoned, "I want you to remember what the letters of your school stand for. Y is for *young*. Young men of Yale can shape their destiny. A is for *ambitious*. Ambitious men of Yale can always win. L is for *loyal*. Loyal sons of Yale, yours is a sacred trust. And E is for *earnest*. Nothing can stop earnest men of Yale. Now go out there and rip 'em apart!"

As the boys thundered out, Stevens walked to the door just in time to hear one of his tackles murmur, "Whew, it's a good thing we're not the Massachusetts Institute of Technology, or we'd never get the second half started!"

Ed McKeever found himself in the same situation when Notre Dame played Army in 1944. McKeever knew he had to employ desperation measures to win.

He gathered his players together and pleaded with them to win the game for his father, who was seriously ill. This was just a trick on McKeever's part, but his boys suspected nothing. They charged out to do or die for Dad McKeever.

But Army proved too good. They ran up 59 points. At this point, a battered Notre Damer glanced at the scoreboard, saw the score, and groaned, "Geez, guys, McKeever's old man must be dead by now."

Texas schoolboys are also wont to invoke the spirits. Before one of Cleburne High School's big games some seasons ago, it's star player, Jimmy Strickland, called upon his team to kneel for a moment of silent prayer.

Shortly thereafter, the enemy took the kick-off and started advancing steadily toward the Cleburne goal. Jimmy called time out and gathered his mates around him.

"Men," he said, "some blankety-blank didn't pray."

――――――――

The late Bo McMillin was always a stout advocate of the stirring battle cry. To illustrate his point, he would rattle off a long list of classics, including "Remember the Alamo!" and "They shall not pass."

But Bo's favorite belonged to his 1943 Hoosier team, which roared into the Northwestern game bellowing: "Not one soul shall cross this line—either vertical, horizontal, or transverse!"

――――――――

Old Bob Zuppke was also a great hand for pep talks. Against a loaded Iowa team one season, Zup decided to lather up his Illini sophs. "Men," he roared, "I want you to get in there and die for Illinois. Nobody will be taken out unless he's dead. Get that? Unless he's DEAD!"

The inspired Illini played Iowa to a standstill until flesh gave out. Late in the final quarter, a frail Illini halfback keeled over from exhaustion. Zup grapped a sophomore substitute. "Get in there and replace that man!" he ordered.

The youth dashed out—then came right back again. "What's wrong?" shouted Zuppke. "Why didn't you take that man's place as I told you?"

"It ain't necessary, Coach," gulped the youngster. "He's still breathing a little."

———

Johnny Lujack, Notre Dame's all-time quarterback great, could flip a pass or a wise-crack with equal bull's-eye accuracy. During the 1946 Army-Notre Dame game, Arnold Tucker, the Army safety man, intercepted three of Lujack's tosses.

On the train coming home, Coach Leahy drew Johnny aside. "Tell me, John, why did you throw so many passes to Tucker?"

"Coach," Lujack grinned, "he was the only man open."

———

Peahead Walker, the much-traveled mas-termind, has a novel way of picking his backs and linemen. "I just take them all into the woods and turn them loose," he says. "The ones who run around the trees become backs and the ones who run over the trees become linemen."

With less than a minute to play, Florida
was clinging desperately to a 31-27 lead over
Vanderbilt. Haywood Sullivan, the Gator
field general, decided on quarterback sneaks
to kill the rest of the time. Vandy Captain
Faulkinberry slammed Sullivan to the ground
on the first two, getting more desperate with
each passing second.

On the third one, the big Vandy tackle
gave vent to his feelings. "Sullivan," he said,
"I ought to kill you."

Sullivan grinned up at him. "Sorry," he
said, "you haven't enough time."

Before Vanderbilt went out to face power-house Louisiana State in 1945, Coach Bart-ling said this to his Commodores:

"Boys, all I ask of you is to be relaxed. We have everything to gain, nothing to lose. I want you to go out there with just one idea —to have FUN."

Dick Bachman got into the game early in the second period and promptly began running into brick walls. Every time he got the ball, a couple of Tigers would smother him. They skinned his nose, cracked his back, and stepped on his chest.

Finally, Bachman turned to end Doug Malsberger: "Are you having fun up there in the line?"

"Well, sorta," Doug replied.

"Then let's swap positions," Dick pro-posed. "It's serious as h - - - back here!"

They're still mumbling about the South-west Conference tackle who approached his coach one evening and asked for $750 to go to a movie. "Seven hundred and fifty bucks to see a movie?" snorted the coach. "Are you crazy?"

"Well," explained the player, "it's a drive-in and I don't have a car."

Westchester (N.Y.) County's most colorful football official was big, witty, good-natured "King Kong" Klein, the former NYU athletic great. At a football officials' meeting one evening, Klein was stressing how important it is for the referee to check with the other officials before signaling a touchdown. "Before throwing your arms up," cautioned the King, "make sure that no official has called a penalty."

"Suppose the players are in your line of vision and you can't see the other officials shaking their heads?" asked a young official.

"As far as our Westchester officials are concerned," retorted Klein, "you don't have to *see* them shaking their heads. You can *hear* them!"

Pudge Heffelfinger, the Yale immortal, and Fritz Pollard, the Brown star of 1916, once appeared on a radio show. After the broadcast, Pudge told Pollard, "I saw you play once. You were the razzle-dazzle kind. In my day, I'd have broken you in two."

"Shucks, Mr. Heffelfinger," Pollard drawled, "you couldn't have even broken my stride."

Stanley "Coach" Woodward, the former Amherst gridder who became the peer of football writers, was once asked to help get a boy into Amherst. A friend described the boy as a four-sport high school star—immense, fast, lion-hearted, and tireless.

"If you can get him into Amherst, he'll be the greatest star they ever had," the guy declared. "Do you think he can get in?"

"How's his Greek?" Woodward inquired.

"Heck," snapped the other, "who cares about his Greek? He *is* Greek. It's his English I'm worried about."

———

There are hundreds of rib-tickling tales about the famous Carlisle Indians. One of the funniest of these concerns an episode in the Pennsylvania game of 1911. At a crucial moment, the referee called for a measurement for first down. It was close but Sweet Corn, the great Indian guard, sighed hopelessly and walked away. He was a Sioux, and his folks had been slain at Wounded Knee.

"How can we expect white man to give us three inches of ground," he sneered, "when white man slew the buffalo, stole the Black Hills, and destroyed our families?"

For a complete switch on the Indian legend, there's the one about Jim Thorpe. It seems that an opposing lineman was giving Thorpe the "business." Thorpe took it good-naturedly until the opponent took a bite out of his leg. Then the great Indian tapped the fellow on his helmet.

"Look, mister," he said, "how about cutting out the kneeing and butting and biting? *I'm* supposed to be the savage."

Rex Enright's eyes bulged in mock horror when, just before his South Carolina team was to meet Clemson, he was asked if Clemson had a big team.

"Big!" he drawled, "Why, those boys are so big that every time they run out on the field they tip it to one side!"

Red Blaik, Army coach, and Billick Whelchel, Navy coach, were standing in a corner of the Army gym back in 1943 as the Navy players started coming out on their way to Michie Stadium. As each passed by, Whelchel would tell about the terrible injuries which the individual had suffered. He piled it on, rattling off a long list of charleyhorses, fractures, sprains, abrasions, and contusions.

"There's one other man I'd like to point out to you, Red," he said, "but I don't see him. He must be dead."

The Yale-Georgia game was one of the country's classics back some years ago. One season the Elis traveled to Athens and took a fearful lacing. Returning on the train that evening, a disgusted Yale rooter stumbled over the feet of Fred Linehan, the Bulldogs' All-American guard.

"Where you goin'?" the unhappy rooter snapped.

"I'm not going anywhere," mumbled Linehan.

"Oh, another Yale back," grunted the other.

In his first four seasons at UCLA, Red Sanders' teams finished third in the Conference once and second three times. He lost out two years ago when the Bruins bowed to Stanford, 21-7. Asked to explain it, Red replied: "Just look at those Stanford players—Kerkorian, Manoogian, Essegian. And now they've got cohesion."

Frankie Albert, the retired 49er, was the speaker at a father-and-son dinner. After his speech, he answered all the questions thrown at him by the kids. One boy kept raising his hand until he finally caught Frankie's eye. "And what's your question, sonny?" asked Albert.

"What's next on the program?" the kid said.

———————

The sophomore quarterback raced into the game with strict instructions to run the team. In the first huddle, he expressed himself in this fashion: "Coach says I'm in charge and not to take guff from any of you seniors. Get it? I'm the boss, you listen to me."

Then he lapsed into a deep silence, trying to think of a good call. Finally he looked up. "Anybody got any suggestions?"

———————

Don't stop driving when you're hit,
Keep on crawling, never quit;
Use all your tricks and squirm-ery,
And I'll see you in the infirmary!

Officially Speaking

ONE OF THE MOST BEWITCHED, bothered, and bedeviled gentlemen on the football scene is the official. These poor guys are subjected to a lot of indignities. But they're not completely defenseless. Many of them are armed with razor-sharp wits that cut and bite.

Football's fabulous referee, Jim Durfee, was a squelcher supreme who slaughtered anybody rash enough to cross him. One afternoon Milan Creighton, coach of the Chicago Cardinals, started needling him from the sidelines. Durfee refused to be baited. Toward the end of the game, he caught Creighton illegally shouting instructions to his players.

Durfee tooted his whistle and paced off 10 yards against the Cardinals.

"What's that for, Jim?" roared Creighton.

"That's coaching from the sidelines."

"You don't know what you're doing," bellowed the Cardinal coach, "and that proves it. The penalty for illegal coaching is 15 yards."

"I know, Milan," said Durfee pityingly, "but the kind of coaching you do is only worth 10 yards."

———————

The great grid ref, Tiny Maxwell, arrived in town one morning to officiate a big game. A bad stutterer, Tiny hesitated to ask his way to the stadium. Time flew by and Tiny became desperate.

Finally he grabbed a kid hurrying by. "L-l-listen," he stuttered, "I-I'm t-trying t-to find m-my way t-to the f-f-football stadium. C-c-can you t-t-tell m-me how t-t-to g-g-get there?"

The boy shot one look at the hulking Maxwell and took flight. Tiny gave chase and caught him after a long run. "What d-d-do y-you m-m-mean b-b-by running away w-when I ask y-you a c-c-civil question?" he demanded.

The boy swallowed. "I d-d-didn't w-w-want t-t-to get m-my b-b-block knocked off!" he answered.

Tiny Bobie Cahn took an intense pleasure in squelching George Halas. One afternoon in Detroit, Halas and the Lions' mentor, Potsy Clark, attempted to play hide and seek with him. They kept sneaking up and down the field, hiding behind the light towers while flashing instructions to their squads.

Bobie, noticing these childish shenanigans, called for time. Motioning with his arms, he summoned George and Potsy from out of hiding to the center of the field.

"Dr. Livingstone," he said, "meet Mr. Stanley. And now get back to the bench. From now on, you get 15 yards every time you move!"

———

To go unbeaten and gain lasting fame,
Better not schedule Notre Dame!

———

Harry Robb once incurred the Pittsburgh Steelers' wrath by penalizing them time and again. Finally Chuck Cherundolo, the Steeler center, couldn't restrain himself. After a five-yard penalty for offside, he blurted out: "Robb, you stink!"

The official didn't say a word. He just picked up the ball and marched off another

15 yards. Then he looked at the burning center and said, "How do I smell from here, Cherundolo?"

———————

Before turning to baseball, Warren Giles, the National League prexy, was quite a well-known football official—known not only for his refereeing but for his snappy repartee.

One afternoon the Nebraska coach, Ernie Bearg, put him on the spot. A Cornhusker halfback had plunged into the line near the goal but had dropped the ball. Bearg thought his man had scored a touchdown before he fumbled. Giles ruled otherwise.

Bearg charged onto the field and stormed, "How far over the goal does a man have to go to get a touchdown, *Mister* Giles?"

"With or without the ball, *Mister* Bearg?" Giles retorted.

———————

The late Tom Thorp, perhaps the greatest of all grid officials, frequently made his own rules. But he surpassed himself on one occasion. Tom was a very religious person who could not stand blasphemy or foul language in any shape or form.

During the game in question, one player

kept growing more and more profane as the action grew hotter. Tom pleaded with him to be careful of his language. But the pleas fell on deaf ears. Finally Tom could stand it no longer.

"You're out of the game," he ordered.

"What rule did I violate?" heatedly asked the player.

Coaches and players gathered around the official. "What rule did he violate?" they asked with growing insistency.

Tom stared at them coldly. "The Golden Rule," he said.

———————

Eddie Dooley, the old Dartmouth All-American, once read about an *official* who scored a touchdown on a 50-yard run with a forward pass. Sorely puzzled, Eddie hopped into his car and rode 500 miles to the official's house. "Jones," he said, "I just read where you scored a touchdown. I can't understand it. I always thought officials were neutral."

"Well," Jones answered, "it was this way. There I was on the 50-yard line with the ball coming straight at me. In front of me lay an open field. Eddie, I had played three years at Harvard and that was the first time I had ever been in the open with the ball! I just couldn't resist the temptation."

Of course, the officials don't win all their verbal exchanges with coaches. In the course of the 1941 championship play-off between the Giants and the Bears, Ben Sohn, a Giant guard, had his jersey ripped off his back.

Out charged Coach Steve Owen with a claim of holding. But the officials turned a deaf ear to his protest. Owen glared at them balefully.

"Maybe I was wrong," he grumbled. "I guess the Bears didn't hold Sohn and rip his shirt off. It must have been moths."

————————

Every coach with a midget halfback owns a reasonable facsimile of the next story. Its hero is Eddie LeBaron, the mighty College of the Pacific "peanut" and former pro great.

Like most small men, Eddie hates to be patronized. And he takes keen delight in chopping big fellows down to his size—both on the field and off. His first day at the training table found him sandwiched between two giant tackles.

The waiter approached and asked one tackle how he'd like his steak. "Rare, red rare," growled the giant. "How about you?" inquired the waiter of the other tackle. "Just singe mine a bit—I want the blood dripping," husked the fellow.

"And you?" asked the waiter, turning to Eddie.

"Well," drawled the unfazed atom, "never mind the cooking. Just turn the bull loose and I'll rip off a hunk as he goes by."

———————

At a sports luncheon in Massachusetts, the local coaches were trying to impress a Southern writer named Dixie Johnson. One of them told Dixie how Bump Hadley, former Yankee pitcher and an ex-Brown U. athlete, once kicked a 54-yard field goal in a high school game. "Now," boasted the Northerner, "don't tell me a Southern schoolboy ever did that."

"That's nothing," answered Dixie. "Back in the days when the posts were on the goal line, we had a boy who stood in his own end zone and drop-kicked the ball over both goal posts—a 110-yard kick."

"Nonsense!" roared the Yankee. "That's not in the record books!"

"Well," drawled Dixie, "y'see, it was illegal. The boy didn't have any shoes on!"

When Columbia broke Army's victory streak in 1948, it was end Bill Swiacki who did the Lion's share of the damage with impossible catches all over the lot. This moved sportswriter Bill Heinz to observe: "That boy Swiacki catches passes the way the rest of us catch colds. He knows where he gets some of them, and the others he just picks up in crowds."

———

Failure to punt cost Colorado its game with Utah, and Coach Jim Yeager intended to see that history wouldn't repeat itself. Before the next game against Brigham Young, Yeager inked across the seat of Center Don Brotzman's pants: "For heaven's sake, punt!" Colorado won, 48-0.

———

After Eddie Anderson's first Iowa eleven beat Purdue by the odd score of 4-0, Anderson explained to a sportswriter, "Well, we had 'em licked with that first safety, but we wanted to run up the score!"

Kingsley was drubbing Anthon High school, in Iowa, 40-0. With Kingsley once more in possession on the two-yard line, Anthon called time out. While taking his breather, a freckle-faced Anthon kid turned to the referee, Honie Rogers, and asked, "How much time is there left?"

"About two minutes, sonny."

Red sighed, "Gosh, I don't believe we've got a fighting chance!"

Red Dog Play

One of those husky corn-fed Iowan school-boys made a trip to Ames to consult the Iowa State officials about a job if he should decide to matriculate. The Cyclone Athletic Director thought the lad might also be a football prospect.

"Did you ever play football?" he asked the young giant.

"Nope," retorted the boy, "but the team always liked to have me around after the game when the fight started."

Halfback Richie, calm and cool,
On the gridiron, no one's fool,
Took a chem test, got a zero,
And thus became a great ex-hero.

Minnesota was playing Northwestern, and there had been 35 fumbles. Dick Hanley, then head coach of Northwestern, ordered a backfield sub to warm up. The lad ran along the sidelines and was then tossed a ball. He fumbled it.

A spectator promptly bellowed: "Send him in, Hanley, he's ready."

PRO STUFF

THOUGH pro football is a rock 'em and sock 'em affair where 250-pound whales are banging into each other on every play, it still manages to come up with a scoreboard-full of laughs. Star scorers in the grin-touchdown column are such fabulous old pros as George Halas of the Bears.

During a kick, a Chicago Bear tackle messed up his assignment and the ball caught him squarely in the seat of his pants. It was recovered by an opposing guard who ran it over for a touchdown. George Halas promptly yanked the tackle out of the game. After the culprit had taken his place on the bench, Halas came over and kindly asked, "How are you, fella?"

"Why fine, coach," answered the tackle, surprised and touched by this concern.

"Good," murmured Halas, "for a while I was afraid you might have concussion of the brain."

Though Joe Sulaitis never went to college, the big Giant back became one of the greatest blockers in pro football. It was the Chicago Bears, led by the mighty Bronko Nagurski, who taught him the facts of pro life. Joe was backing up the Giant line as the Bears came out of the huddle. Nagurski, in the fullback spot, grinned at the babyfaced rookie across the line. "Take it easy on an old man," he pleaded.

He then took the center snap, and crunched through the line straight at Joe. He flattened the rookie with such violence that Joe lay there stunned. Feebly he struggled to his feet, just in time to have another Bear bowl him over.

"Stay down, Kid," growled the kindly ref, "before you get killed."

During the war years, Giant coach Steve Owen had only two players and nine eaters. The worst of the big eaters—a fellow who consumed huge quantities of food—did practically nothing on the field to pay for his upkeep. But he tried so hard that Steve didn't have the heart to fire him. Things went from bad to worse, and Steve finally had to apply the axe.

consumed huge quantities of food—did practically nothing on the field to pay for his upkeep. But he tried so hard that Steve didn't have the heart to fire him. Things went from bad to worse, and Steve finally had to apply the axe.

A master of diplomacy, Owen broke the news to the heavy-eating player in this fashion: "Buddy, I have some bad news for you. They broke your plate in the kitchen, so I'll have to let you go."

———————

Shortly after Bernie Masterson joined the Chicago Bears, George Halas sent him into a game just as the Bears obtained possession on their own 20-yard line. The papa Bear gave the cub quarterback specific instructions: "Run the first play through right tackle, the next around left end, and then punt."

The first play over tackle picked up 30 yards and put the Bears on the mid-stripe. The next play around end was even more successful, giving the Bears first down on the enemy's 15-yard line. Masterson, ever obedient, then punted into the centerfield bleachers!

That Pro Football Touch

And when the Great Maker writes your name,
He won't ask who won or lost the game,
But what was the attendance?

———————

Fans who saw Charlie Trippi's snaking 75-yard punt return in the 1947 pro play-offs, swear that Trippi covered at least 105 yards on that trip. One of the highlights occurred when Charlie stopped short in front of the Eagle bench to let a would-be tackler fly past and land at Coach Greasy Neale's feet.

Neale, by this time, was feeling no pain. He leaned forward and stabbed the frustrated tackler with an icy stare. "Get up, sweetheart," Neale snapped. "He'll be back in a minute."

———————

During one of those old-time Chicago Bear-N. Y. Giant battles, the Giants had but one good scoring chance and that immortal, Ken Strong, booted a field goal. But wait! The Giants were offside. No goal.

Steve Owen, the Giant coach, had watched the line play and was surprised to see Joe Kopcha, the Bear guard, on his knees. Playing opposite him was Steve's little two-ton brother, Bill. And Bill hadn't made the slightest gesture toward Kopcha.

From five yards farther back, Strong again attempted a field goal. Once more he made it. But once more the Giants were offside and Bill left Joe, still on his knees, alone.

So Strong tried again and made it. Steve Owen instantly yanked Bill. "What's the matter with you?" he roared. "You had Kopcha set up for a clean shot and you never laid a shoulder on him!"

"I just couldn't do it, Steve," sheepishly answered Bill. "Every time Ken got ready to kick, Kopcha dropped to his knees and said, 'Please, God, don't let him make it.' And, gosh, Steve, I couldn't smack a guy when he was praying, could I?"

.Taking Out the Interference

When Lone Star Dietz coached the old
Boston Redskins, he always liked to mastermind the game from the press box. One afternoon against the N. Y. Giants, he called
his boys together and instructed them to
kick off to the Giants if they won the toss.

Then he started up that mile and a half
ramp to the press box. Just as he opened the
door, he looked back and saw the Redskins
lining up to receive. Dietz hopped onto the
phone and started raising cain with the Boston bench. "I told you to kick off," he bellowed.

"We did kick off, Coach," came the reply.
"The score is now 7-0."

One of the best of George Halas' vast fund
of rib-ticklers has as its hero that Chicago
Bear immortal, 230-pound tackle George
Musso. One afternoon Musso was flattened
by a terrific block. Trainer Andy Lotshaw
dashed onto the field, while a stretcher crew
poised for action on the sideline.

When Lotshaw reached Musso, he found
him just regaining consciousness. "How do
you feel?" anxiously inquired the trainer.

"Okay," replied the mammoth tackle. "But
how's the crowd taking it?"

When that great all-time pro end, Bill Hewitt, was traded by the Bears to the Philadelphia Eagles, he set up a keen rivalry between the clubs. The first time Hewitt faced his old teammates, the Bears attempted to discourage him as quickly as possible. They sent three blockers against him on the first play. Hewitt hit the ground, but bounced right up again and scornfully surveyed the prone Bears.

"Three men on one end!" he sneered. "What's the matter? Haven't you any confidence in yourselves?"

After graduating from Tennessee with All-American honors, "Bad News" Cafego became the workhorse of the Brooklyn Dodgers pro club. Playing against the Giants one day, Cafego brought the ball upfield practically by himself. Just before the half ended, he broke away over left tackle.

First one man hit him, then another. But "Bad News" kept going. Finally, about five Giants ganged up on him. They wrapped themselves around him, and still he plowed goalward. At last he started down—just as the timer's gun exploded.

"By gosh!" a spectator shouted. "They had to shoot him to stop him!"

A Switch in Time

IT'S DIFFICULT TO TRACE the origin of these stories. Some are based on actual incidents. Others are dis-figments of a coach's imagination. But one thing is certain: if the story is any good, it will get around faster than a rumor.

What's more, it will often be given a switch to suit the style of the narrator. For instance, take that nifty about Bronko Nagurski. The big bad Chicago Bears were needling their star with questions on how he grew up to be so big and strong, and how he kept in such wonderful shape.

The Bronk said he got that way plowing fields. They all hooted at this, pointing out that everyone present had plowed at one time or another. To which the Bronk replied, "Without horses?"

Now that isn't a bad story. But it's merely a variation on an old Bernie Bierman theme. The original has Bierman divulging the secret of his powerhouse Minnesota lines.

"When I see a farmer in a cornfield," the Gopher coach used to say, "my first question always is, 'Which way is town?' If the farmer points with his finger, I drive on down the road. But if he lifts the plow and points—well, we can always find him a job."

———

Back in the days when Fritz Crisler was coaching at Princeton, he once brought an undefeated team into Cambridge for the annual game with Harvard. The night before the contest, Fritz attended a little gathering of Harvard people. When he left, he said: "Good night, gentlemen, and may the best team win."

One Harvard professor was shocked. "You mean, of course, the 'better' team, don't you, Mr. Crisler?"

"No," answered Fritz. "I mean the 'best.' I figure on using three of them tomorrow."

———

Navy's ex-coach, Eddie Erdelatz, could always manage a grin. Early one season, he remarked on the tremendous burden imposed marked on the tremendous burden imposed on the boy who tries to carry both a football and an academic course at either of the service institutions. It was ever so much more difficult, he said, than anything he had experienced in college.

"Well, what did you take at St. Mary's?" he was asked.

"The morning paper," Eddie said.

En route to Litchfield, Illinois, to speak at a high school banquet, Burt Ingwersen had to pull up at a garage when his motor began to miss very badly. The mechanic inspected the car carefully. "Sounds bad," he said. "It will take two or three hours of work."

Ingwersen groaned. "Can you fix it for me tonight? I have to leave for Bloomington early in the morning."

"Sorry," answered the attendant. "I'll have to fix it tomorrow."

"Look," said Burt, "I'm the line coach of the Illinois football team and I have to be at Bloomington to speak tomorrow noon."

"Oh, so you're Burt Ingwersen? Well, I saw the Ohio State game last week, and I sure as heck will get you out of town tonight!"

Some years ago Cornell started to march on Columbia. The Big Red was bowling over the tackles and Columbia's coach, Lou Little, called on one Machinski to go in and stem the tide. As the Columbia spotter high in the press box saw Machinski get off the bench, he phoned down, "Put Machinski on the phone." He then began delivering an essay on tackle play.

Poor Machinski had to stand in front of 30,000 people holding a telephone. Nobody in the crowd knew what it was all about until a leather-lung bellowed: "The poor guy's saying goodbye to his mother!"

———

The boy broke into the coach's bedroom in the football dormitory. "Coach," he screamed, "the house is on fire!" The coach grabbed his bathrobe and dashed up the stairs to the team quarters. Hopeless confusion met his gaze. Thirty boys were trying to jam their way down the single fire escape. A sheet of flame lapped at their heels.

It was then the coach proved he was a real football coach and a leader of men. He lifted his voice and bellowed, "First team down the fire escape—everybody else jump!"

Fumble-itis cost Oklahoma the 1952 Notre Dame game. "We had a lot of trouble holding on to the ball," Coach Wilkinson moaned. "In the first half, our fumbles kept us in the hole and messed up our offense. When we came out for the second half, we had to pause on the steps until our band finished its routine on the field.

"While we were waiting, the Oklahoma drum major threw his baton into the air— and missed it when it came down!

"A nearby fan looked at me and snapped, 'Hah! I see you coach the band, too!'"

————

During the war, Iwo Jima was infested with quite a few Japs who had been exposed to an education in the United States. They were tricky devils who had a habit of yelling advice in authentic Americanese, and any Marine foolish enough to listen paid with his life.

One such Jap, fully armed, came running toward a line of Marines yelling, "Don't shoot, I'm from Ohio State!"

A leatherneck quickly drilled the Nip, remarking, "That's too bad, bud, I'm from Michigan!"

During the intermission of the game between the Chicago Bears and the Army All-Stars back in 1942, the announcer introduced Luidmila Pavlichenko, Soviet sniper credited with 309 Nazis. Next, the man at the mike introduced one of her countrymen, a sharpshooter who "got 150 Nazis with 152 bullets."

At this a voice floated out of the bleachers, "What ja do with the other two bullets, ya bum ya?"

"I" Formation

It seemed the boy had played three years of varsity ball and had never gotten into a game. In the locker room after the last game, he was downhearted. His girl friend, who was waiting outside, had traveled 900 miles to see him play and he hadn't an honorable bruise to show her. Lost in thought, he stumbled against the training table. A bottle of arnica fell over and drenched the back of his pants.

Oblivious to it all, he walked out to meet the g.f. Suddenly he felt a trickle down his leg. "God," he prayed, "I hope it's blood."

———

The big fullback had only two dinners that day, and he gazed with envy at a big sirloin steak that had just been put in front of his teammate—the right tackle.

"Don't tell me," pleaded the fullback, "that you're going to eat that huge steak alone?"

"No," said the tackle, tucking his napkin carefully under his chin. "With potatoes."

To Be Perfectly Frank

FRANK LEAHY, retired Notre Dame coach, is another of Knute Rockne's boys who can lay 'em in the aisles when the spirit moves him. Before taking over at Notre Dame, Frank taught blocks and tackles at Boston College for two seasons. He left with an enviable record and a collection of refreshing anecdotes.

At the drop of a demi-tasse, Frank will tell about the time B.C. went south to play Tulane. The boys had no desire to refight the Civil War, as northern teams frequently have had to do. So when Chet Gladchuk, one of two co-captains for the game, met Captain O'Boyle of Tulane, he made a speech.

"Mr. O'Boyle," he said, "before we toss the coin I would like to tell you our line-up. I play center and am of Lithuanian extraction. At one guard we have Zibilsky, who traces his ancestry to Poland. At the other guard we have Kerr, an Irishman. Manzo, Italian, plays one tackle, and Yaukoes, one of my countrymen, plays the other.

"Goodreault, a Frenchman, plays one end and in the backfield we have, among others, Toczylowski, Polish, and O'Rourke, who was born in Ireland.

"Now what I'm trying to drive home, Mr. O'Boyle, is this: While we all have the interests of the country at heart and admit to a little sectional pride, our grandpappies weren't here when the late regrettable war between the states was fought. Therefore we request that you and your teammates will not hold us responsible."

"It's okay with me buddy," quoth O'Boyle, "I'm from Gary, Indiana."

———

B.C. went south again the following year to play Tennessee in the Sugar Bowl. Late in the game, Bob Foxx, the great Volunteer back, broke loose and was headed for a touchdown. But big Chet Gladchuk tore up from behind and nailed him with a ferocious tackle.

"You-all certainly thumped me hard that time," Foxx gasped.

Big Chet looked around. "You-all heck," he grunted. "I got you myself."

Frank Szymanski, the former Notre Dame football center, was once summoned to appear as a witness in court. He swore to tell the truth, the whole truth, and nothing but the truth.

"Are you on the Notre Dame team this year?" the judge asked.

"Yes, your honor."

"What position do you play?"

"Center, your honor."

"How good a center are you?"

"Judge," exclaimed Szymanski, "I'm the best center Notre Dame ever had."

Coach Leahy was astonished at this burst of arrogance, since Szymanski had always been considered the most modest of athletes. "How could you ever stand up in public and make a statement like that?" he asked.

"It was a bit unusual," agreed Szymanski, "but you see, Coach, I was under oath."

During the heat of a lively session on the "sucker shift," Lou Little turned to Leahy. "Frank," he said, "let's suppose my Columbia team is playing Michigan State. We kick off and State returns the ball to our five-yard line. On the next play, they pull the shift. Wouldn't you say that the shift was designed to pull my team off-side?"

Leahy thought for a moment. Then he replied, "Lou, if your Columbia team kicked off to Michigan State and they returned the ball only to your five-yard line, all I'd have to say is that your defense certainly must be improving."

————

No Notre Dame rival ever caused Frank Leahy more embarrassment than his smallest boy. It seems Frank's papa-in-law was visiting them and the little boy kept begging the old gent to come play football with him.

Grandpa made excuse after excuse, but to no avail. Finally, in desperation, he snapped, "Son, I don't know anything about football. What makes you think I do?"

"Well," piped the youngster, "Daddy said yesterday that when you kicked off, we could get a new automobile."

————

When the 1945 Notre Dame eleven started east for its big game against the powerhouse Army team, a Fighting Irish alumnus who had been trying all week to convince himself that Notre Dame had a chance, came to the station to see them off.

One by one the players stopped at the newsstand and bought something to read. One got *Time,* another *Harper's,* a third bought *Life,* another took *The Atlantic Monthly*—the sort of magazines that learned people read.

Finally a snaggle-toothed guard came by and picked out four comic books. The alumnus beamed, "Thank heaven," he said, "We've got a chance after all."

———

Notre Dame teams probably train harder than any other club in the land. The players consider games a holiday from practice, and Coach Leahy did nothing to disillusion them.

One afternoon he stopped a tackle and asked him how he felt. "I feel pooped," the boy said. "Push yourself, lad," Leahy replied. "You obviously need a lot of work."

Ziggy Czarobski overheard the conversation and was prepared when his coach asked him the same question. "I feel fine," Ziggy replied, "I never felt better, Coach."

"I'm glad to hear that, Zygmont," Leahy said. "You obviously aren't bothered by work. Run ten laps around the field after you're finished here."

The game between Notre Dame and Southern Methodist had hardly gotten underway when Notre Dame scored a touchdown. A spectator cheered wildly and pounded his neighbor on the back. A few minutes later, S.M.U. scored and the spectator went into another frenzy. This aroused the curiosity of his neighbor, who asked, "Which team are you rooting for, my friend?"

"I don't care which team wins," was the reply. "I just came here to enjoy myself."

"Oh," the questioner sneered, "an atheist."

Skirting the Ends

The first visitor to reach Leahy's bedside after his famous collapse during the 1953 Notre Dame-Georgia Tech game found Frank sitting up. Worried, sick, depressed over what apparently seemed to be a heart attack, Leahy's first question was: "What was the final score?"

His visitor beamed. "We won, 27 to 14!"

"Hmm," murmured Leahy, "so we missed an extra point."

———————

Disgusted with his charges in practice, Leahy called them together and laid down the law: "Look, lads, I'm convinced that before we can make any further progress, we must go back to the fundamentals." He reached over and picked up a ball.

"Now this," he said, holding it up, "is a football. It . . ."

At this point a tackle interrupted: "Please, Coach, *not so fast!*"

———————

The bride was rich and beautiful, the groom a former Harvard All-American with an immense pair of feet. As they knelt before the bishop on their white satin pillows, a snicker ran through the congregation. On

the soles of the groom's wedding shoes, the
ushers had printed in red paint, on the
left, "Down," and on the right, "With Yale."

Every football coach dreams of discover-
ing a superman who will lead his team out
of the wilderness and into the Rose Bowl. So
you can imagine the delight of Coach Hodnutt when he found his dream walking—a
boy who could kick like Groza, pass like
Graham, and run like Caroline.

Since all coaches are masterminds, Coach
Hodnutt decided to keep his discovery under
cover. At the proper moment, he would
shoot the boy in and sweep the opponents
off their feet.

Game after game flew by without a critical
development. The season ended and was
followed by another. And still Hodnutt's
"secret weapon" rode the bench. He sat and
sat—through three seasons and two Bowl
games, awaiting the call that never came.

And so we find him winding up his career
—still sitting—in the Rose Bowl. And then
it happened. The invincible machine suddenly fell apart and blew a two-touchdown
lead. The great moment had arrived.

Hodnutt turned to his superman. "Son,"

he said, "get in there and show 'em how the game should be played. There are a couple minutes to go and we need a touchdown to win."

The greatest unknown player in history jerked off his hood with one swift motion—then slumped back on the bench.

"Coach," he moaned, "I can't go in. My legs are asleep!"

———

Leaving the stadium after losing by a big score, the unhappy coach was collared by an old grad. "How many students are enrolled in our university?" asked the o.g. politely.

"About 17,000," replied the coach.

"Is it asking too much to put two of them in front of a ball-carrier?" snarled the old grad.

———

Black Hills Teachers College was taking a shellacking from Nebraska State Teachers College. A sub fullback who thought very highly of himself was sent in for Black Hills, and the Yellowjackets' quarterback called upon him to carry the ball three times in a row. He lost yardage on every play.

Each time he complained about his teammates not opening a hole for him. On the fourth down, he was called on to punt. As luck would have it, he got off a bad one which struck Captain Malcolm, the center, squarely in the back.

The big, slow-spoken Scot straightened up: "What the heck, Kep, do you want us to open holes for your punts, too!"

The ball-carrier soared into the air, turned over three times, struck the ground, and lay still. Everybody in the stands gasped. It looked like a sure fatality. The priest sitting on the bench rushed out, knelt by the boy, and started administering the last rites.

In the middle of the service, the boy feebly opened an eye. He looked at the priest and, with great pain, slowly shook his head. "Stop, Father," he gasped. "You've made a mistake. I want the priest for the *offensive* platoon."

When one of Moon Mullins' boys started nodding during a squad meeting, Moon would always tell a story about Jim Crowley at Fordham. It actually happened at a skull session before one of the Ram's big games against a tough Pitt team.

A second-stringer dozed off, and Crowley threw an eraser at him. The fellow jumped up, startled, and Jim said, "You better stay awake, Joe, because if you don't I'm going to start you against Pittsburgh."

———————

Whenever you talk about one-sided football games, the grandpappy of them all—Georgia Tech's 220-0 whacking of Cumberland back in 1916—comes to mind. George Allen, former commissioner of the District of Columbia, quarterbacked the Cumberlands and he likes to tell of the time he fumbled. As three Tech ogres bore down on him, he saw a nearby teammate shy away from the loose ball.

"Pick it up!" Allen yelled.

"Pick it, my foot!" grunted the other. "I didn't drop it!"

———————

Finding himself in a strange town with time on his hands, the visiting football coach decided to explore the local insane asylum. An attendant took him up to the first floor, marked "Mild Cases." The coach noticed a figure kneeling on the floor with hands clasped in prayer. "Who is that?" he asked.

"Oh, that's a football coach who applied for a job and didn't get it. His mind just snapped. But he'll be all right in three or four years."

The visiting coach was next escorted to the second floor, where the more severe cases were kept, and then up to the third and fourth floors. Finally he arrived at the top floor, where the most violent and incurable cases were quartered. There in the center of the room was a wild-eyed fellow, roaring: "Drive! Hit 'em hard! Keep your head down! Keep those legs moving!"

"What happened to this guy?" the visitor asked.

"He," answered the attendant, "is the guy who got the job the fellow downstairs missed out on."

At practice one day, Moon Mullins' fine fullback, Don Doody, messed up a couple of plays and Mullins really began to give him the works.

Finally Don spoke up: "Listen, Coach, I know you don't think I'm smart, but after I hit 'em a couple of times they'll be just as dumb as I am."

Lynn Waldorf says it was rugged line play that kept California among the undefeated in 1948.

John Cunningham, the big end, was a terror on defense. After watching John smash a dozen Wisconsin end runs, Coach Waldorf asked him to describe his technique.

"Well," John said, "the second the ball is snapped, I charge into their backfield."

"Yes?"

"I grab a handful of backfield men."

"Yes?"

"I toss 'em off one by one till I come to the one with the ball."

"Then?"

Cunningham grinned. "I keep him."

———

The Columbia frosh, playing their first game, had instructions that if the opening kickoff went into the end zone, they were to let it roll over, not try to run it out. The kickoff went to Lou Kusserow over the goal line. He grabbed for it, fumbled, recovered, fumbled again, snatched up the ball, and started to run.

On the bench, Lou Little turned to his assistant, Buff Donelli. "Get that feller outta there," he spluttered. Meanwhile Kusserow was weaving in and out of the enemy, and went all the way for a 105-yard touchdown!

Little reached for Donelli's arm. "Let him stay in," he said. "If we take him out now, we might shake his confidence."

―――――――

The first and second string Michigan State teams were indulging in a full-scale practice game, and Coach Duffy Daugherty was unhappy. His varsity seemed sluggish. They just couldn't get moving. As Duffy turned to speak to an aide, the official penalized the varsity five yards.

"What's that for?" Duffy snapped, when he turned back to the game.

"For backfield in motion," answered the official.

"Good!" enthused Duffy. "That's the first motion anybody's been able to detect in our backfield all afternoon!"

Hick-man Overboard!

FOOTBALL LOST ITS POET LAUREATE when massive-mind Herman Hickman passed away some years ago. Big, genial Herman was a tremendous storyteller. In his team's sickness or health, he could always manage to dredge up a ruby.

Though Hickman is immortalized as one of football's greatest guards, actually he played guard only one season at Tennessee. He started as a tackle. The turning point came in the Alabama game in 1930.

Before the game, Coach Neyland gave Herman his instructions: "Get a yard and a half across the line and make a pile."

So Herman began making piles. But Alabama won, inflicting the only defeat suffered by Tennessee in Herman's four years at the school.

After the game, Neyland came over to Hickman and asked what happened. "I did

73

just what you told me," Herman declared. "Got a yard and a half across the line and made piles."

"I told you to make piles," Neyland groaned. "But I didn't tell you to be at the bottom all the time!"

———————

Levi Jackson, the Yale captain, was practicing his punting. With almost every kick he would yell "left" or "right" or "short." Three times in a row he yelled "short."

"Hey," hollered Coach Hickman. "Don't give me too many of those short kicks, Levi."

Jackson grinned. "Coach," he said, "only time you really got to worry about is not when I holler 'short' but when I holler 'back'!"

———————

Though he became a Connecticut Yankee, Herman would revert to form under stress. Like the Xmas night at Miami when the All-North and All-South teams started out for the football stadium. The bus with the Southern squad was in front, with the bus carrying Herman's Northern team bringing up the rear and catching all the fumes.

Hickman finally stood up in the aisle and

ordered the driver to shoot ahead of the other bus. "Come on," he bellowed, Let's get ahead of those damyankees and stay ahead of them for the rest of the night!"

He turned back to his players and encountered a chilly silence. One of the players chided, "Coach! Coach! *We're* the damyankees!"

Nonplused, Herman strode back down the aisle and roared, "Come on, come on! Let's get ahead of those damrebels!"

After steering the North eleven to a victory over the South All-Stars, Hickman was installed in a $100-a-day suite in a swank Miami hotel with free run of a $60-a-day cabana on the beach. Herman stretched out in the hot sun and puffed contentedly on a 50-cent stogie. He flicked off an ash and drawled:

"Ah wonder what the losin' coaches are doin' today?"

I think that I shall never see
A fullback bigger than a tree;
A tree that may in autumn wear
A dozen tacklers in his hair!

Hickman combined a quick wit with a mountainous appetite. Which sometimes made for considerable frustration. Once he was invited to a fashionable banquet where his hostess' table consisted only of the daintiest portions of delicately cooked snacks. After the meal, a great hunger still possessed large Herman.

As everybody rose from the table, the charming hostess came over to the guest of honor. "I do hope you will do me the honor of dining here again soon," she gushed.

"Sure," boomed the famished Hickman. "Let's start now!"

———————

Hickman always insisted on promptness at Yale. The first time he called one of his famous dawn conferences, one of his aides arrived late.

"Gentlemen," declaimed the poet laureate of football, "I might as well inform you now that there are only two excuses for anybody being late at these meetings. They are sickness and death."

Herman's eyes then lit on Stu Clancy, an assistant coach who worked as an embalmer during the off-season. "And I mean private, not *professional*, deaths!"

Accustomed to public speaking since infancy, Hickman could handle alumni as easy as splitting an end. He blandly assured the old Blues that he could have won a great deal oftener than he did but that he didn't want to set any standards that might be difficult to live up to.

His aim, he said, was to lose just often enough to "keep the alumni sullen, but not mutinous."

Boxing a Tackle

After college, Hickman joined the Brooklyn Dodgers pro footballers. The owner of the club, Shipwreck Kelly, also played in the backfield. When the Chicago Bears came to town, Kelly and Hickman drew a tough assignment. They were supposed to take out Bill Hewitt, the Bears' very tough end.

Shipwreck took a good look at the bulky Bear, patted Hickman on the shoulder, and said, "Go get him, son. *I'm* the owner of the team!"

———

Herman was a mighty tough guard in his college days at Tennessee. After a game with the Volunteers, the Dartmouth coach asked one of his tackles, "How tough was that Hickman?"

"I tell ya, Coach," replied the tackle. "He called me a damyankee and I pretended not to hear him."

CONZELMAN CUT-UPS

NO collection of football humor is complete without a chapter on Jimmy Conzelman, the smoothest, wittiest tale spinner of all. After giving up the teaching of cross-bucks and reverses, Jimmy became the world's most popular after-grid-dinner speaker.

A typical piece of Conzelman whimsy may be found in his classic reply to Dr. Hutchens' charge that the connection between athletics and moral principles is dubious and that the college athlete is led to believe that everything, even slugging, is done for the alma mater.

"Dr. Hutchens is right," said Conzelman, who was coaching Washington University at the time. "Down at Washington we don't permit such slugging. Oh, perhaps a little crack here and there, but nothing soul-stirring or ecstatic. Our team simply isn't built ring or ecstatic. Our team simply isn't built for slugging. But we find biting very effective. Biting doesn't need size and certainly not much speed.

"One of the finest guards I have ever coached was Biter Jones, a young fellow with a splendid undershot jaw that gave him an advantage once he got hold. Biter Jones made a great record at Washington. Besides placing three years straight on the Missouri Valley All-Star Team, Biter Jones bit eleven guards, two centers, and a flanker back. He only lost 65 yards through penalties. The only criticism he ever got was when the Sigma Chi fraternity broke his pledge for snapping at a house mother."

———

The biter must have had a blood-brother at N. Y. U. For in one game a Violet lineman was penalized twice for biting. In practice the following Tuesday, the coach caught him biting one of the scrubs. He stopped play and shook his head worriedly.

"That's a bad habit you've got there, Baron. We'll have to do something about it."

"I got an idea, Coach," interjected "King Kong" Klein, the Violet's All-American tackle, "let's just play him on Fridays."

Conzelman is also something of an image breaker. To the twittering of the idealists that football develops the ability to take orders and submit to discipline, Jimmy gives the back of his hand. It seems he once had two co-captains, Zibby and Droke. Zibby, although the quarterback, never had much to say, while Droke, the halfback, was cocky, garrulous and persuasive.

In the big game of the season, Conzelman instructed Zibby to call play number 80—a good scoring bet—when the team reached the 20-yard line. The occasion arose in the second quarter. The team went into a huddle —stayed there longer than it should—and when the boys finally ran the ball it was a number 14 play. They lost six yards and the quarter closed without a score.

Between the halves Conzelman yelled at Zibby, "Where was the 80 play? Didn't I tell you to call it when you got downfield?" Zibby waxed apologetic, "Well, Coach, I guess it was my fault but I really did call number 80. But you know how Droke is. He's always talking and when I called '80' he checked signals and told me to call '14.' "

Conzelman told him to be commanding and sent him out for the second half with the ter, with the score 6-0 against them, Conzelman's team again reached the 20-yard-line. Here's where we win, he thought. Watch that 80 play go.

The team went into a huddle and stayed there and stayed there, to emerge finally and run—a 14 play! The boys lost ten yards this time, the game was over and the irate coach hustled to the dressing room to call on Zibby.

"What's the alibi this time—where was the 80 play?" he roared at the boy. Zibby hung his head. "Coach," he almost cried, "I called that 80 play at least ten times. Each time Droke checked it. He wanted the 14 play. I had to let him have his way, I was afraid we'd be penalized."

By this time Zibby was dressed and he pulled a dime out of his pocket, flipped it up two or three times and said, "Gee, I'm thirsty. I'm going down to the corner for a Coke."

"What have you there, a dime?" asked the coach. "That's enough for two bottles. Bring me a Coke, too. A good cold bottle, for I'm all burned up after watching you listening to Droke all afternoon."

Zibby went away and came back in five minutes with two bags of salted peanuts in his hand. "Where's my Coke?" the coach yelled.

Zibby turned his head away. He couldn't look his coach in the eye. Finally he said, "I met that fellow Droke again."

———

Jimmy Conzelman prided himself on his ability as a character builder. At a testimonial dinner to one of his St. Louis U. teams, he praised his eleven for its high moral qualities. An alumnus followed him on the dais and sought to enliven things a bit by relating a few of Jimmy's undergraduate escapades.

Inspired by what he heard, the next speaker remarked, "Darned if I don't believe it takes a guy who never had any character to teach it!"

———

During the last quarter of the 1916 Georgia Tech-Cumberland debacle, won by the Rambling Wrecks, 220-0, one of the Cumberland players came out of the game in a daze. As he staggered toward the wrong sideline, the coach asked him if he was all right, if he knew where he was.

"Sure, Coach," the boy replied, "I'm on the Georgia Tech bench. I been in the game four times and I ain't going back!"

The first day of practice, Gale Sayers received a kick five yards back of his own goal and dashed 105 yards through the entire Kansas first team.

More chagrined than elated, his coach called Gale over and pointed out his mistakes. He had run away from his interference, had zigzagged more than necessary, had carried the ball in the wrong hand, etc. etc.

Sayers listened quietly, then casually asked: "And how was she for distance, Coach?"

———

MOUSE TRAPPING THE TACKLE

The coach of a high school team in the West heard about an unbeaten team in Pennsylvania and inquired about a post-season game. "We haven't lost a game in three seasons," wrote the Westerner.

"So what?" the coach from Pennsylvania scornfully replied. "We haven't had to punt in five years!"

———————

When Ike Armstrong gazed at the 16- and 17-year-old hopefuls who turned out for his wartime Utah U. team, he wondered how he was going to pick a first team. He rubbed his chin. That gave him an idea.

"All boys who shave step forward," he barked. Eleven boys stepped out, and Ike had his first team.

———————

Monk Simons, the ex-Tulane coach, once walked into the locker room of one of those small Southern colleges, just in time to hear the coach's final instructions:

"When we git ready to punt and you hear that ball go boom, you go as fast as you can and flatten whoever gits the ball on the other side. But if you hear the ball go boom, boom, turn around and git on that ball without fail."

After a certain coach reported back to his athletic director that his team lost a game because the line wasn't charging enough, the director squelched him with the comeback, "They're charging more than we can pay 'em right now!"

———

When Harry Stuhldreher coached Wisconsin, one of his critics wrote a letter suggesting that Harry be replaced by two high school coaches—Eary Wilkie, of Edgemore Academy, and A. J. Barrett, of Madison East.

This letter infuriated Harry's son, Skippy, who played quarterback for Madison West. Skippy swore he'd write a letter in return. "No," his Dad said. "That won't do. On this job I've got to take this sort of thing. And you've got to take it, too."

"I won't take it!" Skippy shouted. "Why, my coach at Madison West, Willis Jones—he's the guy who should get your job!"

Out-of-this-world Wit

COLGATE WAS STEAM-ROLLING over Hamilton back in 1909. Desperate measures were called for, and Coach Buck O'Neill singled out a sub. "Miller," he snapped, "go in for Doyle at center. Move around, play anywhere you think they'll strike. But stop that running attack."

Miller rushed in and obeyed orders to the letter. He moved from side to side, making tackle after tackle. Colgate was stopped cold, and Hamilton went on to win. As Miller walked off the field, Coach O'Neill rushed over to him. "Great game, boy!" he enthused. "Once you got in there, our defense sure stiffened."

"Coach, I've got something to tell you," Miller answered bashfully. "Doyle never came out."

And then there's the one about the dim-witted safety man. With the score tied and one minute to play, he awaits a high booming kick. He carefully gauges the arc, then suddenly starts tearing up the field, letting the ball bounce behind him. He sidesteps, pivots, whirls, throws off imaginary tacklers, as he runs—unmolested, of course, to the enemy goal. There he turns and starts trotting back to midfield.

As he passes his frothing coach, he chirps happily, "Nice touchdown, wasn't it?"

"You ape!" the coach screams. "You can't score a touchdown without the ball!"

The moron stops dead in his tracks. "Darn it," he moans, "every year new rules!"

After a tough game against Georgia, Charley Justice was invited to a dance at an exclusive country club. He soon found himself tripping the light fantastic with a cute little thing whom he had not met formally. A little self-conscious, he said, "I'm afraid my dancing isn't very good this evening. I'm a little stiff from football."

"I think you're very nice," retorted the girl warmly, "and it doesn't make the least difference to me where you come from!"

Several seasons ago, the St. Luke's High School team of Ho-Ho-Kus, N. J., was taking a pounding in a scrimmage with a nearby team. Back after back had to be helped off the field. The coach finally had to insert his last remaining halfback. Realizing that the boy was a bit dense, the coach decided to check his assignment on the next play—an end sweep. He looked at the sub and asked, "What do you do on this play?"

The boy looked him straight in the eye. "I do my best, Coach."

———

At a senior dance, the recently demoted varsity quarterback, upon mention of the coach's name, began taking the coach apart right down the line. The sweet young thing at his side smiled and said, "Do you know who I am?"

"Why no," replied the athlete.

"I," she said, "am the daughter of the coach."

The athlete paled. "And do you know who I am?" he stammered.

The girl admitted she didn't.

"Thank heaven!" he murmured, rushing out into the night.

Between halves of a game at Colgate University, the visitors' band marched out on the field, played a couple of peppy numbers, then lined up in front of the Colgate stand. There followed the usual shifting around of musicians as they prepared to spell out something for the Colgate fans.

When the word was finally formed, however, it spelled out PEPSODENT.

Making a shoestring tackle late in the game, one of the defensive halfbacks smashed his finger. The team doctor rushed him into the dressing room, where he bandaged the injury.

"Doctor," moaned the player, "when my hand heals, will I be able to play the piano?"

"Of course you will," assured the doctor.

"You're a wonderful doctor," said the happy player. "I never could play the piano before."

The Giants once beat the Redskins, 14-7, without making a first down! In fact, they chalked up exactly one yard by rushing!

"One yard!" sobbed George Marshall, the Redskin owner. "I can make more yardage than that just by falling down!"